The Fear Book

Facing Fear
Once and for All

Zen Center
POBox 91
Mountain View, CA 94042

Monastery/Retreat Center
POBox1994
Murphys, CA 95247

Keep It Simple Books
-Publisher-

ISBN 0-9636255-1-9

For those who have faced the fear
and for those who will

Special thanks to:

-Monique and Brian
-All those in workshops and retreats who willingly explore the process of fear with me
-June Shiver for turning all this material into a book... once again

WHAT FEAR IS

In the process presented here for dealing with fear, fear is the hunted, not the hunter. Fear is the quarry you must stalk and confront and unmask, to reveal to yourself that all that separates you from yourself is an illusion.

Fear is not what you think it is.

Fear is not who you are underneath your facade. Fear is not the real you that you must somehow fix or improve or overcome

Fear is a very useful signal along the path to freedom. The stronger the fear, the closer you are to what you are seeking. If you want to stay "safe" (i.e., stuck where you are), fear tells you to stop what you are doing. But if you want to be free, fear lets you know you are on the right track, it is a signal to push ahead in the same direction, to pick up the pace.

Avoidance of Life

Student: I've been thinking that I'm not really a fearful person; fear just isn't that much of an issue in my life. And I don't see a connection between fear and my concern about what is a serious issue for me, overeating.

Guide: You could go somewhere where the eating would be taken out of your hands, and you could see a lot of things about it.

Student: Well, that's one thing that keeps me from going on retreat, that

I can't choose when and what I'm going to eat.

Guide: This is fear. Some of the things we may not think of as fear—anger, sadness, irritation, urgency, depression, control issues— are pointing to underlying fear. So if you hear yourself say you don't like not getting to decide what and when you eat, look underneath that and see if there is some panic about not being in charge.

4

Resistance is one of the processes that masks fear.

"I don't enjoy swimming / dancing / parties / cities / camping / group discussions / travelling..."

"I'm not interested. It's not my kind of thing."

"I've done that already and don't need to prove anything by doing it again."

"I would love to, but I tried, and I just can't."

"I'm taking care of myself by staying away from this thing I know I'm not ready for."

"I'm not afraid, I just don't want to."

"It's dangerous."
"It's silly."
"It's boring."

Every time we choose safety,

we reinforce fear.

When we try to avoid the discomfort
that we call fear, our world grows
smaller and smaller...

We find ways to avoid
    people
    activities
    circumstances
    experiences
that might cause us to have the
reaction we fear.

                  As we get older,
we become afraid of more and more.
                      We close down.
                      We close off.
                      Our lives shrink.

When we attempt something new and find ourselves feeling really uncomfortable, we believe the discomfort means that something is wrong, so we try to get out of the situation. As time goes on, we learn to get out sooner and sooner and sooner, until we move directly to avoidance, even before we consider doing something that might be scary.

Can you list things you used to enjoy but no longer do because they are too scary?

· DRIVING ON FREEWAYS
· MAKING NEW FRIENDS
· TAKING RISKS

HOWEVER, there are things —
    like falling in love —
that we do precisely because they leave
us sweaty of palm, short of breath,
and weak of knee.

(A lot of advertising promises that
same breathless thrill: go there, buy
this, wear this, and then you'll feel
that way.)

                    The irony is that
even when we pursue those desirable
feelings,
our world still shrinks!

Whether we are:

avoiding all that could produce the
dreaded discomfort we call fear, or

pursuing all that could produce the
desirable feeling we call excitement,

we are removed from the present
moment by the belief that our lives,
our selves, will be the way they should
be only in
    some other time and place,
    some other alternative
    to what is
                here
                        and
                                now.

The relentless pursuit of happiness
is one definition of suffering.

The single-minded avoidance of pain
is another.

I knew a woman who was convinced
that her happiness consisted in marrying
a wealthy man. Nothing in life
interested her except wealthy men, and
her world became small and exceedingly
unhappy.

Our world shrinks when we are
paralyzed by fear of making mistakes,
fear of doing something wrong.

But if we simply take a step and see
what happens,
our world opens
a little bit.
Then we can
take another step.
Every step enlarges our view; every
thing we do shows us something.

As the old Zen masters say:
When we are willing
to pay attention,
everything enlightens us.

A friend used to say to me:
   "I'm afraid I'm not going to get a
   job."
   "I'm afraid of being alone."
   "I'm afraid I'll run out of money."
The list went on and on.   I would
try to help her address each fear until
I realized that we were dealing with
problems that did not exist.   The
constant was "I'm afraid," which could
be followed by an endless series of
purely imaginary difficulties.

Only when we focused
on the <u>process</u>
rather than
the <u>content</u>
could we begin to address
what was really going on.

We could talk
for hours,
days,
lifetimes,
about what is wrong,
    what could happen,
    what won't work.

	JUNE					
S	M	T	W	T	F	S
				1	2	3
4	5	6	7	8	9	10
11	12	13	14	15	16	17
				21	22	23	24
				28	29	30	

Don't do it.

Instead, take a step. Look around
see where you are, and see what your
next step will be. Take that step,
see where you are, and the next step
becomes clear. Maybe it's back to
where you started—

                  you cannot know
until you get there. Each step is
clear only from where you are at the

moment; the "final" step is not apparent at the beginning— only from the step immediately before it.

Each step
is part of a learning process,
and since no matter what you do,
you will learn something

there is no way
to make a mistake.

There is simply no _reason_
to be afraid.

Sitting around
thinking about
what won't work
is like a
scientist

deciding the result of an experiment
beforehand— not a way to learn
anything.

If we really want to know how
something is, or what is possible, we

P l
    u
     n
      g
       e
              ahead.

We might not find what we thought
we would find,

        but we'll find something.

Life is a creative process,
and creativity has to have that
WHOLEHEARTED ABANDON
of
PLUNGING AHEAD—

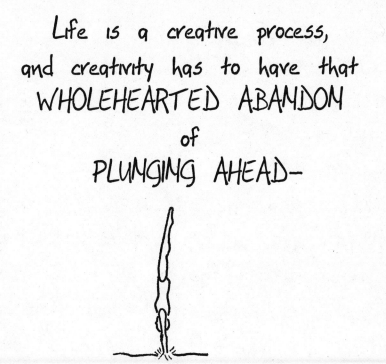

taking the next step in the knowledge
that we will learn something.

It is not possible to make a mistake.
We cling to the idea of making a
mistake to maintain the delusion that
we can know what cannot possibly be
known— what hasn't happened yet.

Fear of Fear

The Sensations of Fear

Several years ago while visiting my daughter and my first grandchild, who was then a toddler, I decided to build a fence around the backyard so my grandson could play freely and safely outside. I had only a few days for the project, my daughter had no tools or supplies, and it was summer in Georgia (90 degrees Fahrenheit and 90% humidity), so I knew it would be a challenge. But I also knew I would rest easier 3000 miles away at home if I could picture Brian with a secure play area.

I began early and worked late.

We made frequent trips in their little car for boards, posthole diggers, and dozens of things I hadn't considered before I took on the task.
And we had fun,
with everyone,
including Brian,
helping out.

The last evening before my flight home, we made the big push to finish. By working until dark (about 9:00pm), and a few hours the next morning, I figured I just might finish. We had to go into town for a couple of last-minute items, so to save time, we had a fast-food dinner

By 10:00pm everyone was in bed. I was having a cup of tea when I began to feel anxious. My first thought was that perhaps there was someone outside the house; maybe I'd heard a noise and was responding to it even though it hadn't consciously registered. I peered out of every window, closed the curtains, turned on the exterior lights, and went back to my tea.

The anxiety grew.
I could feel that I was headed for what is called a panic attack. My brain was searching, scanning, scrambling frantically to figure out the cause of

this momentary hysteria. I was covered in a cold sweat, my heart was pounding my breath was approaching a pant. I tried to focus my awareness on breathing to calm my body down.

"What is this? What's wrong?" I asked myself. "If this is a premonition, then we are very near the end — the missiles must be on their way. No, that's crazy. But what is it? Am I worried I won't get the fence finished? Ridiculous! I could always postpone the flight. Am I worried the plane will crash? That's not it. What is it?"

In a few minutes, I was in the bathroom, sicker than I had ever been.

Dinner exploded from my body. Finally, it came to me: I had food poisoning.

My stomach was churning, my mind was racing, I was cold, clammy, weak. Since I had never been poisoned before, my mind had no experience of this, and so it went to the only experience it knew that could explain these sensations. "This is fear; something awful must be going to happen." But those sensations had nothing to do with fear. The sensations were my body trying to expel poison. Not only did my explanation to myself not prevent something from happening, i.e. getting sick, but by focusing on something purely imaginary, it took my attention away from what was actually happening.

"Without fear, wouldn't you just walk out into traffic?"

The belief is that being afraid keeps you from doing something dangerous or just dumb. But that's one of the processes fear uses to protect itself.

When we look more closely we begin to see— especially if we decide to approach something we are afraid of— that fear is protecting itself against us.
It looks as if fear
is on your side,
taking care of you,
keeping you safe,
UNTIL YOU DECIDE TO DO
SOMETHING IT TELLS YOU
NOT TO DO.

At that point you become enemies; you
are in an adversarial relationship with
that which supposedly is protecting you.

In other words,
rather than simply being a signal that
something is going on,
fear begins to look like
an active force
with an agenda of its own.

One might conclude
that fear itself
is the danger.

ONE

You are home alone.

It is the middle of the night. A sound from another room wakes you. You lie in bed with your mind scrambling for an explanation. Nothing fits except that someone has entered the house.

Your stomach is knotted,
your palms are sweaty,
your breath is shallow,
your heart knocks in your chest

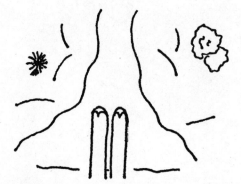

You are at the top of a ski slope.
You look down and what you see is
steep and icy.

Your heart pounds,
your breath is shallow,
your stomach is in knots,
you break into a cold sweat.

THREE

Early evening, and you have cooked dinner for someone you recently met, who turned out to be the most wonderful person in the world. The very person, in fact, you've been waiting for all your life. It's fifteen minutes before your guest arrives. As you make a final check of the house, the meal, and your appearance,

your palms are clammy,
your stomach tightens,
your breathing quickens,
your heart...

Three very different situations.

First, a prowler in your house, which could be life-threatening.

Second, physical activity you have not only chosen but have paid a lot of money to do.

Third, an emotional experience you have dreamed of and wished for.

The physiological responses are very similar in each case, but how we think and feel about the situation— whether it is acceptable or not— determines whether we label the experience "fear." In the case of the potential romance, we might call the experience excited anticipation; on the ski slope, it could

be exhilaration or thrill; hearing a
prowler, we might call it terror.

If we can simply be with whatever it
is that is being experienced—
    the pounding heart,
    the tight stomach,
    the sweaty palms—
there is no problem. Those sensations
do not mean that you should or should
not do anything.
        They don't mean anything at all.

But when we feel threatened, we
believe those sensations mean that
something terrible is going to happen to
us, something that we cannot stand,
and we extend that to mean
we will die.

In fact, nothing has happened to us that we did not survive.

The fear of fear
shrinks our world.

We will do anything to avoid the discomfort of fear even though we have <u>never</u> examined the experience itself, <u>never</u> taken a step toward it and looked to see exactly what it is, <u>never</u> considered that it might not mean what we think it means.

The Emptiness of Fear

Much of what we call fear is thought.
For example, a car swerves out of
control in front of you, and everything
goes into slow motion. Adrenaline
rushes through the body at the moment
of danger, and evasive actions are
taken to avoid a collision. In that
moment there are no thoughts, there is
just a oneness with the situation.
Instead of thinking about what to do,
there is just doing the next thing.

Many people report that in situations
when they are truly threatened, there
is no fear. The whole experience
arises in each moment — there's turning

31

the wheel of the car, there's stepping on the brake — but there is no experience of anyone doing it, of making conscious decisions.

I consider this phenomenon some of our best evidence that fear
    does not help us,
    does not protect us,
    does not take care of us.

"Fear" comes in afterwards.

<u>Only later</u> there are thoughts of what <u>might</u> have happened.

"The car almost hit us."
"Another few yards, and we would have gone off the road."
"I could have been killed."

In fact, none of those things happened. All that happened was sensations and thoughts about those sensations.

What most of us think of as fear is primarily a mental process of imagining situations that do not exist in the moment.

WHERE FEAR COMES FROM

Student: I am going to a dinner party
with some people I don't know very
well, and I'm worried that my hands will
shake like they always have at times
like these. I know this could be an
opportunity to be compassionate with
myself whether I'm shaking or not.
But I say, maybe not yet, maybe not
with these people. I go back and
forth with it. I think I'll go; no,
maybe I'll take one of my pills so I
won't shake.

Guide: Do you consider going and
shaking?

Student: And just not eating the soup?
"Just don't serve me soup, please."

Guide: You are trying to avoid an
experience that could be helpful for you.
What if you turned this around?
What about going with an attitude of...

Student: Hoping they serve soup?

Guide: Yes, and telling yourself that this
could be really interesting. Otherwise,
the underlying message is that these
other people are more important than
you are. For the part of you who is
afraid, it's one more bit of information
that what these people think is more
important than her feelings. No wonder
she is afraid.

Conditioning

How has it happened
that we live much of our
adult lives in a
strait jacket of fear?

Children don't know there is anything
to be afraid of. Up until around age
five or six, children are not particularly
self-conscious, they aren't awkward,
they don't think in terms of something
being wrong with them.

There was a time for each of us
when we were confident and capable
and open and eager to learn to do
new things. In the process of being
socialized, that was destroyed. We

were taught to leave ourselves and
focus on others, and we were
warned and
cautioned and
threatened into near paralysis.
We received little support from adults
for our
confidence and
capabilities and
eagerness to learn and explore—
because they never had that support
themselves.   We grew to feel
inadequate and insecure and anxious, and
by projecting that onto our own children
                    we pass along the fear.

To make the transition
from our early sense of complete
adequacy and fearlessness
to
living freely
and functioning well in the world,
we needed support
we did not get.

Instead, we were given the assumption
that fear
is what keeps us safe.

In fact,
Intelligence is what keeps us safe.

At the age when most kids learn to ride a bicycle, safety isn't really an issue for them. They aren't yet thinking there's any danger because they're not clinging to life the way we have learned to. They don't look at activities from the point of view of what terrible thing might happen; little kids don't imagine that they might spend the rest of their lives in a wheelchair. But a child who wants to learn to ride a bicycle can't get the simple information he or she needs without big doses of other stuff: how they're not doing it right, and what could happen if they do it wrong.

All of this comes at a child in a way
that is hard to grasp, except for the
message:

> there is something
> to be afraid of.

The child doesn't know exactly what
that is, but can hardly avoid concluding
that his or her adequacy is part of
the problem.   After receiving so much
of that kind of information, a child
simply won't try new things that bring
up those feelings.   It is just too
scary.

Instead, what if someone just taught
the child to ride the bicycle without all
the warnings and threats and anxiety?
Not assuming that he or she should
already know that streets are dangerous

or know how to handle a bike around cars, dogs, kids, other bikers? (How would a little kid know all this?) What would be helpful is for someone to explain it all, all the subtleties and nuances — not as if the child is stupid or careless or headed for disaster — but simply by way of giving information to someone who doesn't have it.

(Notice how commonly information is passed on with an attitude of disdain, with the implication of someone's inadequacy, in a tone of voice that says, "What's the matter with you that you didn't already know that?" That's how we were spoken to as children, and we are largely unaware of such subtle put-downs when we speak this way to others.)

Another way of describing what happens to children is that they're going along completely involved in their experience of the moment, with no illusion of being separate from anything, when somebody yells at them that they've done something wrong. They're jolted out of their natural ease and confidence and plunged into the awful energy of an adult's anger and fear. Suddenly they're being told that they've done something wrong; they're yanked away from their own experience into a nightmare of confusion. The underlying message is that paying attention to ourselves, to our own world of experience, is wrong, and that to be safe, we must turn our attention to others.

This happens again and again, until we have our own repertoire of voices cautioning us and warning us and threatening us, reinforcing the idea that we cannot be trusted with ourselves. "You should have known better." "What's the matter with you? Can't you do anything right?" "This is too hard for you." And now we replay those messages to ourselves internally, incessantly undermining our own adequacy.

What we need for that transition from the innocent mind and heart of the child to an adult who can function well in the world is someone who knows the ropes, who can tell us how things work, who can guide us lovingly from not knowing through becoming capable and confident with whatever arises.

For most of us,
that is what was missing in our lives.

Student: Here's one: I sit down to work and fear comes up. "What if it's no good?   What if I can't do it?"

Guide: Well, let's suppose you had just sat down to work and I walked up and said, "What if that's no good?   What if you can't do it?"

Student: Hmmm.   I think I'd wonder why you were saying that.   I think it would make me mad.   Who do you think you are, questioning my ability?

Guide: Okay.   If someone "outside" of you expresses a belief in your inadequacy, it would make you question their motivation, it would make you angry that they would even think such a thing. But if someone "inside" you expresses the same belief in your inadequacy you go to what you call fear.

Student: That sounds like it.

Guide: Good. Now where in that is the fear? I'm right here with a lot of BELIEFS, a lot of IMAGINARY EVENTS, but where is the fear? Even if you were not successful with this whatever it is that you're currently working on, do you believe that that will result in humiliation? rejection? Will you wind up on the street living out of a shopping cart? Will you not be able to survive the event? What is going on?

Student: I don't know. I just know that when that voice suggests that I'm going to fail, it's like an icy hand grips my heart.

Guide: And that's the "fear" that rules our lives. Someone says something that implies that something is going to happen to me in some future time and place, my body is filled with sensations, and I'm conditioned to believe that means
  something about who I am,
  that I should do something,
  that I should not do something,
  a general "there's something wrong and
    I'm in big trouble."

That's a lot of being jerked around by one little voice asking one little question.

But if we never examine it closely enough to see that it's a little conditioned voice programmed to ask anxiety-producing questions, we will remain convinced that it is the voice of God threatening us with imminent destruction.

Spiritually it is essential to understand
that there is nothing
in fear that is
helping us.

Someone who lives at another Zen
center was telling me how she spent
last winter in terror because she was
getting close to just dropping everything
and being in the moment.   She would
get right to that point,
she could see that
being in the moment   TERROR
was freedom,
    and all that was there was terror

Now, what is that TERROR?

It is egocentricity
losing its grip on you.

You were taught that
fear is useful,
that it takes care of you.

So,
when you began to let go of it
a part of you
feels like it is dying
and it doesn't want to die.

It would rather you died.
It would rather your world shrank
until there was nothing left of you.

If you no longer believe
what fear tells you,

you will live
and it will not.

That is a point on the spiritual
journey that
almost nobody gets past.

When that TERROR arises,
when it gets backed into a corner
and it is a matter of
its survival
or yours,
almost nobody has
the required
combination of
courage, desperation, willingness—
to stand up to it.

When this force in you that has
controlled and motivated you all your life
is screaming,
   "If you do that
   you're going to die!"
very few people are going to say,
   "Well, I just need to find out if
   that is so."

That's why it is so important to
remember that <u>projection</u> is going on.
What's being screamed is,
   "If you stay with this, I will die."
And that's true: "I" will die.
   Its life is your death.
   Its death is your life.

Fear has its own identity.
The identity of fear
is separateness.
Fear is the movement

away from center.
It is the experience

of being separate.
It is not a position; it's what happens
when you are separate — fear is the
movement, the process, of separation.
When you are out there, away from
center, then fear becomes the identity.
Fear is the "I" that is separate.
The "I" that is separate is afraid.
The "I" that is separate
has been created,
has been born,
will die,
is in grave danger.

Everything is a threat to the survival of that separateness. So we move in fear, and we are fear.

Many of the processes of fear are designed to keep us from seeing how fear is the movement to separation. Fear forces us to spend our lives dealing with · it,
ostensibly to overcome it.
But that is a trick.

Only fear (the illusion of separation) would want us to work to be unafraid, precisely because
it is not possible for a separate self
to be unafraid!

This is a trick to make sure you always exist:

> decide that you want something
> that it is not possible to have
> and then spend your life
> pursuing that.

This is a recipe for egocentricity to live forever because, we might guess, with rebirth the unfulfilled desire will seek form again.

SEPARATION (fear)	NO SEPARATION (No fear)
self	Self
isolation	oneness
abandonment	connection
fear	clarity
deprivation	plenty
anger	forgiveness
illusion of control	letting go
suffering	bliss

(Add your own.)

Student: I remember being a child on our farm and standing near the rear end of a horse and having no fear of that, then someone yanking me back and telling me I should be afraid, never do that again, and so on.

Guide: Something important happened there because fear and being stupid and being somehow bad got all put together. When adults say to children, "What's the matter with you? Can't you see that's dangerous? You know better than that!" then fear and self-doubt undermine the desire to learn. Children believe you when you tell them they should have known better. They're not sure how that works, but they can only trust that you know what you're talking about.

Children are naturally fearless; they are open to the world and to exploring and learning from it. But when they are repeatedly told that something they have done is stupid and foolish, they are humiliated, so that eventually they no longer find new situations interesting. They stop being excited about exploring the unknown, because the unknown has become another opportunity to be wrong.

The child has to be shamed into internalizing the adult thoughts and feelings. In fact, the child is fine, even after she's been jerked away and told that she's crazy and could have gotten killed. But soon the child accepts that she is stupid and needs to be afraid.

But the fear is not of the horse.

The fear is of the adult and the adult reaction. Suddenly the person on whom you depend for survival is very upset. Something is wrong! As a child you have no way of knowing what's going on, but you certainly feel the upset. It upsets you. It "frightens" you. You have just gone in one second from everything being fine to everything is wrong! And it seems to be your fault. Something about the horse—you've done something wrong about the horse and it's bad and dangerous. I suspect that most of that kind of "learning" never got through to us as children. We just lumped the wrong, the bad, the dangerous, and the upset together and attached them to horse.

What you really needed was somebody to explain how to be around the horse or the hot stove or the lawnmower or the sharp knife or whatever — so that you could feel safe and confident as you deal with these things in life instead of being intimidated by them.

HOW TO ADDRESS FEAR

Student: Tomorrow I have a meeting in the city and I'm taking the tram.

It's been years since I've been to the city, and I have to get from the tram station to where the meeting is, which is scary, and I'm also scared about the meeting itself. My whole life I've been afraid of being afraid, of having to go through frightening things alone. So my first reaction was to get somebody to go with me, but that didn't work out. As I have continued to pay attention to this process of fear and self-doubt, I have seen through it. I see it for the fiction it is, and at this point, I'm glad I'm going alone.

It's actually kind of exciting — tomorrow I'll get on the tram alone, go to the city alone, go to the meeting alone. I might even just wander around for awhile. It's still scary, but for the first time it's more like an adventure than a nightmare. I almost feel like the crew on <u>Star Trek</u>, heading off into the unknown.

Guide: That attitude of mind of being present with ourselves is the crux of the matter. It is the experience of not being alone that we've always longed for. If we're present to ourselves, we can drop our ideas about doing it right or wrong and just learn from it all, just to see what happens, noticing how we react and what we say to ourselves and how it feels and what we do in this or that situation.

Student: There is a part of me who doesn't see this as an adventure at all and is truly terrified. Now and then I hear that voice saying I have a date with a bridge — before or after the meeting doesn't matter, except that if I jump before, then I won't have to go through with the meeting.

Guide: The idea is to allow those voices to speak and to turn the attention to them, rather than trying to suppress them. Resisting is the best way to give over all our power to the voices of fear.

Student: Well, there's another part of me saying, You shouldn't have to jump off the bridge. Nothing terrible is going to happen; you'll live through this. You've lived through far worse.

Guide: We live our lives trying to avoid imaginary experiences, but the "something terrible" that is going to happen is already happening! It is the process of trying to avoid something terrible happening. It is a projection: there is nothing that's going to happen to us that is worse than living in this kind of fear. That's as bad as it gets.

When we drop the idea that we're _supposed_ to be having a certain kind of experience and open ourselves to the experience we _are_ having, then we avoid nothing, and we fear nothing, because we are right here with ourselves.

Fear is the experience of being
identified as a separate self.
FEAR and SEPARATENESS
are synonymous.

And yet,
          avoiding fear,
          resisting fear,
          fearing fear,
are greater problems than fear.

If we had learned to believe that the
sensations we call "happiness" meant
that awful things might happen to us,
we would now have the same reactions
to happiness that we have to fear—

          It's not the experience,
          It's the belief!

We often operate out of beliefs.

<u>Hypothetical Example</u>

- I want my boss not to smoke in meetings. I'm miserable and hate it, but I don't dare say anything. Why? Each time I'm in that situation, a series of beliefs plays out just below my conscious awareness. In this case the series is:

- If I say something, she'll get angry.
- She has a lot of power in my life.
- If I anger her, she'll retaliate.
- If she retaliates by firing me, I'll be without work, money, resources, or options.
- I'll be on the street; I'll starve to death or be murdered.
- If I say something to her about not smoking in our meetings, I'll be putting my life in danger.

Realization of non-separation
is the ultimate (and only) "control."

We are desperate to control because
we believe ourselves to be separate,
alone, and vulnerable.
When I am not separate, there is no
one to protect.
I am invincible—I can be defenseless.

The only way to be invulnerable is to
be completely vulnerable,

and

for us to
open to total vulnerability requires that
we go beyond our fears and to know
that we have never been separate
from our true nature, from all that is.

Fear of the "unknown"
is actually
fear of my own imagination.

Many of us see ourselves as victim to fear, as if fear is chasing us through life and we must elude it.

I'm going to get you!

NO! I'm afraid of fear!

I want us to switch this around. We're going to become the hunters and fear, the hunted.

How does fear of fear limit my life?

What is fear anyway?

What are my beliefs about fear?

What thoughts accompany fear?

What physical sensations do I label "fear"?

Question every fear thought.

How do I know that?
Is that true?
Who says so?
Is that my experience or is it a belief?

Look to see how fear
is set up in your mind.

Learn to ask:
Is that happening NOW?
Is that true NOW?
Who says so?

Learn to explore assumption
                    speculation
                    rumor
                    prejudice
                    negativity.

Being negative will not keep the things
you don't want to happen from
happening.

What if we replace those voices that warn and threaten us...

You're just not quite good enough.

They're going to laugh at your suggestion.

You have no courage. Give up.

You can't do it. Don't even try.

Be careful not to make a mistake!

You don't try hard enough.

You are lazy and boring.

You are too loud! Calm down!

with messages that support our inherent adequacy and our growth toward a full and free life?

Go ahead. Give it your best shot. It will be okay.

There is nothing wrong with you.

You are kind and generous.

You are never alone. I'll always be with you.

Your feelings are okay whatever they are.

If we are afraid of fear,
we feed it
and it grows.

If we leave fear to itself,
if we give it no power,
              no energy,
                  (yes, this is possible!)

eventually it consumes itself.

BLISS

Becoming a Mentor to Ourselves

mentor - a wise and trusted counselor
-Random House College Dictionary-

If we can become for ourselves the
mentor we always wished we had, then
everything in life becomes an exciting
adventure.

      We can do all those things
we've always wanted to do but
convinced ourselves we couldn't do. We
can live our lives in the company of
someone who really loves us and cares
about us and supports us in our
natural eagerness to grow and in our
intelligence about how to do that.

If we look at life
as an opportunity to
end our suffering,
as an opportunity to
embrace and heal
all that has happened to us,

our attention moves
AWAY from trying to
fix ourselves and
figure everything out, and
TOWARD being with ourselves
as we live our daily lives.

83

So, within myself, the critical move in
the healing relationship is away from
judgment and self-hate and toward the
place of compassion from which I can
embrace the part of me who is afraid,
confused, uncertain, unskilled.

From the place of compassion, I assist
the small part of me who wants to
explore and
experience and
be successful
in all the situations in which I have
not had any support, in all those areas
I've never explored because I didn't have
anyone with me to help me through
the frightening, difficult, painful places.

Instead of becoming

SMALLER AND SMALLER

as I close my mind and heart against
all that would be threatening or
frightening, my world becomes

LARGER AND LARGER

as I help that small part of me go
forward into life.

This "small part of me" is also the
spontaneous and
excited and
adventuresome and
brave part,
the one who was there before those
qualities were frightened out of me.

When I approach everything
as an opportunity to heal,
there is nothing that will not be
available to me.

If everything new becomes an
opportunity to open the heart of
compassion and embrace in that
compassion all those aspects of myself
that have felt timid and insecure and
threatened, then I will rush toward
the new,
the unknown,
the challenging.

I will seek new ways
to bring me back
to myself

The childlike part of me who was shamed for not knowing, being awkward, "doing things wrong,"

will be excited to have the encouragement and support to try new things.

So, rather than saying to myself,
　　"I can't do that,"
　　"I'd look foolish,"
　　"What would people say?"
　　"It would be a waste of time,"
I can decide to give this excited, enthusiastic part of me all of the life experiences she never got to have.

"I can't"
becomes
"What next?"

Now I begin to accept opportunities to
    meet new people
    learn new sports
    start a business
    speak in public
    build a house
    travel, write, sing—

pursuing with wild abandon

all that brings me closer to who I
always have been.

Because we are most often identified with the socialized child and the socialized adult within us, we get stuck moving back and forth between a child's fear and an adult's fear. But it is possible to find within ourselves a way of experiencing life that was ours before we were taught to be afraid, before we were convinced that life is big and scary and overwhelming, when the world was a place of awe and wonder, when we had boundless energy because there was nothing keeping us from simply being present in the moment.

That's the place we're looking for.

The only thing that can help us move back to the enthusiasm of the pre-socialized child is to come from the place of compassion within ourselves that can embrace the fear of the frightened child and the socially conditioned fear of the adult.

When we come into that compassionate awareness that is not afraid of the fear, that can embrace the fear, we are able to heal the wounds of the child and the adult and begin to live the lives we've always wanted to live.

Student: I have a friend who is terrified of the dark. In bed at night she hears noises and imagines a burglar is about to kill her. She can't sleep. I wonder how being one's own mentor might work in this instance.

Guide: The best opportunities are the ones we cannot avoid. They are our greatest gift and greatest ally, because otherwise we would keep putting things off, and procrastination is another one of the ways fear protects itself. "I know I need to look at that, but not right now. I need to be a little stronger." But our own internal mechanisms keep bringing us into the situation. Often we face it only because we no longer have any choice.

And that's regrettable for two reasons. First, at that point it has all become so serious and so grim that we don't see that it can be interesting and fun. Second, it reinforces our inadequacy.

But if we get to the point of saying, "Yes, this is good, I want to see how this works," we are empowered by that. I'm no longer a victim waiting around until I have no choice, just fighting for survival and praying I live through it all. I become proactive. So in that sense, it's very good to be pushed to your limit so that you no longer can postpone looking at your fear.

If I were your friend
who is afraid of the
dark, the first thing
I would do is make
everything just as safe as I need it
to be. I would check all the locks on
the doors and windows. I would install
an alarm system. If I'm afraid to go
down the hall to the bathroom in the
middle of the night, I'd build a bathroom
onto my bedroom — whatever is required.
The point is to show the part of me
who is afraid that I really am on her
side, and she is finally number one with
somebody. She might still be afraid,
but maybe she won't feel quite so
alone.

What to do next? I might ask her to tell me what she is afraid of, and I would write down her thoughts and feelings, being as specific and detailed as possible. I would ask her to tell me the worst that could happen. I would help her make alternative plans: if this happens, we will do that. If you get too scared tonight, we will go to a hotel.

Every step of the way watching what happens.

Student: You're describing a willingness to go to any length...

Guide: Any length, yes, to take care of this frightened child inside of me.
That is the relationship that is missing.

It has nothing to do
with the content.
She is experiencing
a dramatization of
what it feels like to be abandoned by
my "adult" self. In that sense, she is
already in the hands of a maniac.

Student: So the mentor would be
supporting her through this situation?

Guide: Yes. "Even if somebody comes in
and gets us, we'll be together. We
cannot prevent life, we cannot control
events, but I'll be here with you, no
matter what."

You only have to do this once to begin
breaking down the process of

abandonment and the fear that follows that.

Student: It doesn't matter what you work with?

Guide: It doesn't matter a fig. The content is irrelevant.

Student: Where does the mentor come from? If I could do that for myself, I wouldn't have a problem.

Guide: You can do it, and the quickest way to find that out is to realize that you already know what you need to hear.

If you're interacting with someone close
to you and you want a certain
response and you're not getting it, how
do you know the response you want?
You know
from within yourself.
It exists inside you.
You already know how you want to be
supported and loved and cared for.
You can provide that
for yourself!

If you pay close attention, you'll see
how you stop yourself from receiving
the mentoring that is already there.

In receiving there is an experience of wholeness / oneness / satisfacton.

We focus on DEATION

because it helps us maintain our illusion of being separate,
of needing to get more of something. *

*We never get it because it constantly changes!

Once you establish the mentor relationship with yourself, it feels the way it should have felt in childhood.

You are absolutely safe and cared for and loved and approved of and watched over.

Then you are free to do whatever you want to do because nothing terrible can happen to you. With this sense of safety, you can explore the whole world. Once that mentoring process is in place, you can apply it to anything.

What fear (depression, anger, sadness, etc.) says	What the mentor says

With every fear thought that arises, take a few minutes to do this exercise. It might take a while to find your true mentor, but don't give up. The mentor hasn't given up on you.

The Process

Let's say I'm terrified of dogs, and I'm going to be desensitized. First, I would look at a dog, and then gradually get close to it and eventually touch it and so on. But I'm also afraid of water. And bridges. And heights. And...
The point is to acknowledge that the identity being maintained is fear, because once we see how the process of fear works, it has broad application.

But if we focus only on the content, there's no ability to turn to the next thing we're afraid of and apply it to that.

If we were

just dealing with the fear of elevators,
then we would just throw this person
in and have them go up and down, up
and down until they no longer cared.
But that's not what this is about.
We are attempting to get to the
fear itself.

This is not about

heights or
dogs or
public speaking.

It's about the fear that motivates us
and how we maintain it

Do something you fear,
not to conquer the fear, not to
accomplish a task,

but to familiarize yourself
with the processes

with which fear protects itself.

I encourage you to start with small fears and
then move on to bigger ones.

Never make a contest with conditioning.

If a voice says,
   "I can't. I'm afraid,"

the most helpful kind of response is,
   "It's all right to be afraid.
   I'm here with you. We'll
   take it slowly. It's okay."

And if a voice says,
   "But you're just a coward!"
it is helpful not to argue. It doesn't
matter what someone says. Why
waste your time being defensive? Being
whatever and however you are is fine.
And once you have accepted that,
                the contest ends.

How would I address fear? An example: Let's say I have a fear of heights. I hate to fly. I won't stay above the second floor in a hotel, I avoid bridges whenever possible, I don't hike in the mountains, etc.

What to do?

First, I learn to disidentify from the part of me who is afraid. Until I disidentify from that part and move into the mentor role, I am pretty much incapable of compassionate response.

It is important to note that while I am identified with the part of me who is afraid I am most often not actually experiencing the object of my fear.

It's not as if I'm walking over to the edge of the cliff, peering over, and then feeling the sensations of fear in my body. The <u>mere idea</u> of a cliff sends me into a panic. So I avoid cliffs so that I won't be afraid. Am I really afraid of cliffs? Is that what I'm fearing <u>now?</u> No, there aren't any cliffs around. I am afraid of my feelings. I am afraid of fear.

We rarely experience what we think of
as fear.

What we actually feel
is fear of fear.

ANXIETY
is the fear of fear—
the dread of an experience
I won't be able to stand

The next step is to make peace with
how I'm feeling. For many of us, that
notion is revolutionary. We were taught
that feelings are something to
get through,
get over with,
get away from,
or deny.

I SHOULD BE OVER
THIS BY NOW!

Most feelings are unsettling,
untrustworthy,
embarrassing,
inconvenient,
even dangerous.

I CAN'T BE SUCCESSFUL
IN BUSINESS AND
HAVE MY FEELINGS,
TOO!

So, to make peace with your feelings,
imagine that you are simply going to co-
exist with them. You don't have to
worry about them, or control them, you

don't even have to take them personally(!!). All you have to do is let the feelings be — and if you stay with it, before long, they will let you just be.

How does that work?
You watch your feelings. You have a front row center seat. You don't have to perform — you're the spectator. Remember, you have disidentified from the one who is afraid, and you are prepared to be a mentor, but for now you're just watching.

☆ NOW ☆
PLAYING
MY
FEELINGS

As strange as it might sound,

WE DON'T HAVE TO TAKE OUR FEELINGS PERSONALLY.

It might be helpful to keep a journal of your investigation of a specific fear.

THE ADVENTURES OF JOHN AND THE TEN-STORY BUILDING			
SENSATIONS	THOUGHTS	EMOTIONS	BELIEFS

You could write down what your sequence of steps will be — just imagining the building, then driving there, then going up to it, then going into the elevator and closing the door, then going up to the top, and then finally to the edge.

And you would write down what you wanted to be looking at: the sensations, the thoughts, the emotions, the beliefs.

Now you are ready to address your
fear of heights
  .not to get over the fear
  .not to learn to be all right in high
   places
  .not to change or fix yourself.

You are doing this
to bring
the light of consciousness awareness
to the subject of fear.

You are going to demystify the whole
subject of fear.
You are going to learn to be the
mentor you always wished you had.
You are going to embrace the part of
you who is afraid and has always felt
alone and abandoned and unsupported.

Perhaps,
at the end of this fascinating journey,
you will be relaxed and comfortable at
any height.
Perhaps not.

The result
is not the point.

Compassionate awareness
is the point.

And so you begin. You decide you're
going to go to the top of the ten-
story building. It might take several
stages before you actually go anywhere.
Just sitting and thinking about it might
be enough to bring up the fear.
If so, start there.

You could set up a time each day to work with the fear. Just a few minutes might be enough at the beginning. Do this so that the fear doesn't assault you every time you're not paying attention.

(And notice that that is exactly how it happens! You're right there watching and it's hard to find the fear. Turn your attention away and ZAP! the voices try to scare you to death.)

The procedure is the same each time. You take whatever step will bring up the fear. Perhaps now you drive to the building and sit in your car in the

parking lot.   Just be with whatever
happens.
You are watching,
seeing ever more subtle levels,
really hearing what the voices are saying
seeing the belief systems behind the
voices,
watching your emotions react to the
voices,
feeling the sensations.

It becomes so familiar, you could map
the whole process.

"I do this, then I feel that, and then I say that, and then I feel such-and-such, and then..." Not many mysteries left at this point. It's all pretty predictable stuff.

So, you have become completely familiar with the whole process of fear, and yet the thought of standing looking over the edge of that building still starts the voices shrieking, "I CAN'T!" That's okay We are not trying to make it to the edge of the building, we are finding out about the tyrant named Fear.

Now, remember,

this is a spiritual process, so when we
catch this little beast,
we're not going to
destroy it,
we're going to
embrace it.

We're going to include it
in our acceptance
and compassion.

We're going to
love it
into extinction.

Student: I was hoping to come here today and get some answers, but you keep asking us questions, and all I hear you telling us is the same old thing,

pay attention.

I'm disappointed that that's what it's about. I want to figure out how to get over the fear, and sitting on the cushion doesn't do it for me. I know you're saying there isn't a right way, but I'm convinced there must be.

Guide: The conviction that there is a right way is one of the processes fear uses to protect itself. Since there really isn't a right way, believing there is is a way of staying stuck, not of seeing the fear. It keeps you caught up in looking for the right way instead of looking at what is really going on.

Student: But I don't see what's going on. It sounds exciting when you describe it, but none of that happens when I'm just sitting there, and I get bored.

Guide: It is boring to egocentricity.

Student: I'm getting tired of sitting on the cushion because I don't pay attention most of the time, and this voice keeps telling me I'm doing it wrong.

Guide: What are you doing when you're sitting there?

Student: I'm breathing, I'm trying to see how to disidentify. But really I think I'm waiting for the period to be over, and not paying attention at all.

Guide: What are you paying attention to when you're not paying attention? How do you know you're not paying attention?

Student: I'm thinking of things I need to do when I leave here.

Guide: Ah. So when you're sitting there on the cushion, what you're paying attention to is things you need to do later. And you believe that's doing it wrong because you should be paying attention to something else.

Student: Yes, I should be paying attention to my breathing and the sensations in my body. Isn't that the right way to do it? (general laughter)

Guide: This is really good for all of us because it's that belief system — that there really is a right way to do it — that keeps us from simply being present to what is going on. But we don't see that belief system because we're immersed in it.

Student: I do see that I'm caught in a belief system, because as soon as you said that, I thought, okay the right way to do it is that there is no right way to do it.

Guide: It's not that trying to do it right is the wrong way to do it, it's just that trying to do it right keeps us stuck. If we think, "I have to let go of this right/wrong continuum!" we're right back on it. Finding ourselves caught in this trap over and over can be really frustrating.

Student: Yes, and then I just feel sick of the whole thing.

Guide: And that frustration keeps us in the same place. What the frustration signals — same with boredom — is that we are getting perilously close to seeing

through all this.   Everything needs to
intensify so we will turn our attention
to the frustration itself, the boredom
itself, the fear itself, whatever is
there, and away from the right/wrong
trap.

Student: For me it's more like rage
than frustration.   So should I turn my
attention to the rage instead of the
right and wrong?

Guide: A short cut, at least intellectually,
is to get it that there is nothing
wrong with anything.   It's the
comparisons that keep us stuck.   So if
you want to know what's going on,
turn your attention to that, not
comparing it with some other way it

should be. When rage is there, turn your attention to rage. When boredom is there, turn your attention to boredom. When frustration is there, turn your attention to frustration.

Student: And when I'm distracted...

Guide: Turn your attention to distraction.

Student: I have this theory that everything in me is fear-based or I wouldn't be so desperate to always figure out the right way. I think that if fear weren't driving me, things would just be okay. But my belief is that without fear, I would make a big mess of my life.

Guide: Without fear, things would just be what they are. When we are centered, nothing is personal, so there is no idea of fault or blame or control over what happens. The reason fear keeps such a tight grip on us is that we believe there is a right way for things to be. But we think that finding the right way to do everything will protect us and we won't have to be afraid.

Student: I'm getting excited about this because I think I'm hearing something very different in the whole idea of paying attention. It's not a means to an end, which is the way I've been thinking about it —"if I just pay attention, I'll get an answer"—but it is the end itself. I remember you saying that paying attention is freedom. So I'm getting the sense of living in that process rather than getting something out of it.

Guide: Exactly. Well put.

Student: And so the duality comes together, the process and the content, because paying attention to the content becomes process, and the process itself becomes content.

Guide: "The same eyes with which I see God, God sees me."

Worry, fear, and negativity do not stop life from happening.

Situation	Possibility	Possibility	Possibility	?
"There's no point in asking for a raise I'm sure I won't get one."	You ask and you do not get a raise	You ask and you do get a raise	You don't ask and you get fired for not being assertive.	
"She's in college now, but if I let her have a car, she might have an accident."	You get her a car and she has an accident.	You get her a car and she does not have an accident.	You do not get her a car, and she has an accident on her bicycle.	
"I really want out of our relationship, but if I say anything, I'm afraid he'll be really hurt."	You say something and he's really hurt.	You don't say anything and live in misery.	You say something and he acts relieved.	

It becomes an adventure to see what
happens when I do the thing I fear
and when I don't do it,
watching very carefully:
    sensations → emotions → thoughts → beliefs
        everything about it.

There is a slight little movement and
a whole chain of events is activated.
Where does it start?
What do I believe about this?
What happens if I say yes?
What happens if I say no?
What do I think this reveals
   about me?

I watch myself say, "This is boring.
I've seen this so many times," or,
"I hate this. I don't want to do this."

Watching the same old thing over and over and over,

and eventually realizing
that none of it
means anything.*

*And realizing that when we are present, nothing
is ever "the same old thing".

Student: Most of my fears center around right/wrong, also. Will I do it right? How can I be sure it's right? These questions are fueled by endless replays of all the things I've done wrong. Today I was trying to come back to the moment rather than go with these same imaginary scenes from the future and rehashings of the past. The voices would begin to say things like, "If you don't try to do the right thing, if you're not concerned about understanding how life works, you're no different from an animal. You're no different from that bug down there."

Guide: As if one more beating about something that's past or one more rehearsal for a scene that is never going to happen is going to enable you finally to accomplish the impossible: to know how something is going to turn out before it happens. The ultimate illusion of control.

Once again, if I were to come up to you and begin recounting all of the most difficult periods of your life, pointing out how you <u>could</u> have done that, or you <u>should</u> have done that, or <u>if</u> <u>only</u> you'd thought of that or taken that approach and then coaching you on all the ways you should approach your life in the future,

what would your response be?

Would you think I
   liked you?
   cared about you?
   had your best interests at heart?
I hope not.   I hope you would wonder
what my game was.   What on earth
could motivate me to want you to feel
bad about yourself?   Could it possibly
be a way of gaining power over you?
A way of having control over you?
Very likely.

So, the next time that voice starts
trying to convince you that you should
leave the peace and comfort of the
present moment to wander
around with it in the world
of past or future
calamities, you might

just give it a polite "no, thank you"
and invite it to come sit quietly here
in the safety of this moment with you.

Fear of making a mistake...

From center
there is no such thing as a mistake.
From off center
(illusion of separation)
almost everything
we do, feel, say, achieve

SHOULD BE
BIGGER AND BETTER
THAN IT IS.

"I'm always in a hurry. It feels like everything is urgent. I must work and move as fast as possible or I won't get everything done, and as a result, something bad will happen."

The important thing is to be with the urgency. Instead of letting it dictate what you're going to do to satisfy it, turn your attention around and focus directly on the urgency.

Ask urgency the same questions you would ask boredom and frustration.

Student: For years I have struggled
with speaking in front of groups. I
can force myself to do it, but the
problem persists. I observe and observe
that fear, but I feel I could observe
forever and it would make no difference.

Guide: If the relationship to fear does
not change, it's a clue that we are
not observing what needs to be
observed. It's like watching the
magician's hands and missing what's really
happening.

Also, as long as we're expecting a
particular outcome, it doesn't work. It
won't work to observe the part of me

136

who fears speaking in groups if my motivation is to stop being that way. What I need to know is the _process_ that is at work here. Then it won't matter whether I speak or not.

Generally, when someone has trouble speaking, it's because there was some sort of trauma. Children tend to be naturally expressive until something stops them. So my guess is that there's a part of you who was traumatized and that's just covered over.

What we're doing is seeing how fear protects itself. Surrounding our identity are layers of protection, and we're removing them so we can see how it all works. If you continue to be uncomfortable talking, that doesn't mean something is wrong, it just means you haven't seen what there is to see.

Student: What if I never see it?

Guide: The part of you who asks that hopes you never will. Let's say you

had a child who was kidnapped from your house. You devote your life to finding this child. Someone says, "What if you never find the child?" Wouldn't your response be something like, "What is the point of such a question? I'm not going to quit looking just because I might not find my child. Clearly my chances are better if I keep looking."

It's not that your life is a failure if you don't find the child or a success if you do. You're just looking because the child is missing and finding the child is what you're trying to do. So in the same way, you are looking simply because you are looking.

Student: I'm wondering if it would be good to try to force myself...

Guide: When you have observed the processes involved enough to know what is really going on — what happens physiologically, emotionally, mentally, behaviorally — and you are present to yourself in that situation, you will have given that part of yourself enough freedom that he will speak spontaneously.

You are providing a safe environment for him, so that when he expresses himself, he just expresses himself.

We can break out of the circle of suffering by being for ourselves what was missing when we were children — someone to listen, someone to be there with us as we struggle, someone who accepts us no matter what.

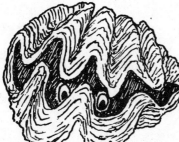

We need to stop taking ourselves personally. We need to see that we are simply human beings, and this is what happens to human beings, this is how human beings operate. We come into the world with the ability to experience ourselves as separate. Our own particular experience of being separate from all that is — the "what" of it, the content — is just another boring little story, except to ourselves.

"I grew up with these people and they did this to me and then that happened and I tried to cope but it didn't work and I became a victim to that..."

We could go around the room and each
plug in our own story about how it
was.   But it's so difficult to stand
back enough from the content to see
the process.

Once I see that this
is just the process of
being a human being,

                   I have a chance
                 of not taking it all
                     so personally.

I didn't create this,
I was born into it,
so why should I spend my life punishing
myself for being a human being?   The
punishment is another process with which
fear protects itself

As long as I am caught in believing
that this is right
and that is wrong
and this makes me a good person
and that makes me a bad person,
I am completely
enmeshed in egocentricity.

Once I realize that this is just a
waste of time, and that duality, the
world of opposites, is simply a way of
staying stuck in suffering,

then I have
a chance of stepping back, of
disidentifying enough to get out of that
system, by not taking myself personally.
Now I can just observe how a human
being operates, see what's going on.

Now I have a chance of moving into
being a compassionate mentor for myself.
There is a motivation to move into
that place to end suffering,
to help all beings.

The fastest way to stay identified is
to be in our heads:
  I don't understand.
  That doesn't make sense.
  What about this?
  What if this happens?
  I need to be careful of that.

Worrying that something terrible might
happen prevents me from noticing what
is already happening, which is that I am
actively maintaining the fear that is
stifling me! It's projection at work
again: the very system I am projecting
out onto other people is the system
that is operating me.

I'm the one who maintains this, and
then I remain a victim to it.

The Ski Slope: Mentoring Myself

I took up downhill skiing to celebrate
my entrance into the sixth decade of
my life. I had many motivations, one
of the primary ones
being a commitment
to continuing to do
new and potentially scary or dangerous
things.

I do this for all the reasons suggested
in this book, and because I work with
people on things that are very scary
to them but are no longer scary to
me. I don't want to lose touch with
being scared because it would be too
easy to forget what it is like to feel
threatened. Becoming an "expert" can

make us insensitive to those who don't
yet have that expertise, and we can
forget that we're an expert only in
our one little
area. Being
a nervous
beginner can keep
the compassion and humility exercised.

I'm always
depressed.

get
over —
it.

My first time out on the slope was
with a friend who, though not a skier,
is an extraordinary athlete. During the
course of the day I wound up in some
places I should not have been in. I
took some bad falls, and generally hurt
myself a lot. I decided lessons were
in order. With lessons, I improved until
I could do well enough to have a good
time.

One day I was skiing with a friend, and my old ski instructor made me a gift of a lesson with the head instructor at the area. "You'll improve dramatically," she assured me. "You're ready for the next level." In fact, I felt no need to improve dramatically, but it was such a generous offer, I overrode that little sense of discomfort that arose with the gift.

It was a disaster. We went high up to a slope that was in deep shade and was quite icy. I was told not to worry about what I had been doing previously, just follow him. Three or four falls later, I thanked him and told him the lesson was over,

and I was going to get down off that mountain the best way I could.
It was a hard thing to say since it wasn't his fault, and I didn't want him to feel bad, I just wanted to get me out of there in one piece. The biggest struggle was not succumbing to the voices who wanted to blame me for not listening to myself when I knew I didn't want a lesson in the first place.

I suspected that was the end of skiing for me. Then, a week or so later, my grandson had a vacation day and wanted to ski. He was nine years old and had skied less than I, so I figured I could probably manage. In preparation,

I gave myself absolute permission to do
whatever I needed. If I wanted to
snowplow all day
(a beginner's tactic),
I would. If
Brian wanted to
go where I couldn't go, I'd find an
instructor to take him. Every second I
was mentoring myself, "It's okay, if you
don't like it, you can quit. You don't
have to do anything you don't want to
do. You never have to ski again if
you don't want to. We'll do whatever
you'd like."

It was the best day of skiing I've
ever had. I skied more and better
than ever before.

The secret

is to disidentify.
This all comes down to not allowing
egocentricity to be in charge.
First we watch how we get
    hooked back
    into the fear. FEAR
Next we watch the process of
    identification as it happens.

Instead of sitting in the audience and
watching the magic show and wandering
how it's all done, I'm sitting in the
front row waiting for the magician to
come on-stage, and I'm looking closely at
everything. Because I'm leading this
investigation — I'm not a victim in this,
I'm the pursuer — I can get up on the
stage, go around behind the magician,

look in from the wings.   No vantage
point is forbidden to me.

I will probably have to go back to that
show again and again,

                    and I will probably
get to see how I get distracted from
my pursuit, how my attention goes
elsewhere, but my aim is to see
every
    single
        thing
            that
                happens.

I'm not doing this for any reason other than wanting to know how it all works.

It's not going to make me a better person.

It's not going to get rid of anything for me.

That's not the point.

The point is that now I am in a different relationship to the fear.

I am bringing
the light of conscious awareness
to the exploration
of the process of fear.

The continent of fear,
of egocentricity,
is out there (in there?)
for you to explore.
When you start out, it's as if nobody
has ever been there before, and as
the first explorer, you can feel a real
thrill.

Being an explorer is not the same as
being a traveler; you are not doing this
to get from point A to point Z; you
are doing this for the sake of
exploration. You just want to find out
everything that is out there in that
unknown ~~terror-tory~~ territory.

If you keep at it, you will know every
tree, every rock, every turn in the

path, because you will have gone over every inch of it, back and forth, many times.

If someone else shows up, you will be able to give them directions, although, of course, we would hope that others would want to see it all for themselves.

You can tell them that over there is this interesting feature, and across there is something no one would want to miss, and once you get to this place it's easier to move on to that place, and the trip up this mountain is long and arduous but definitely worth it.

This is the attitude we bring to the exploration — not "I've got to get to

the other side as quickly and painlessly
as possible and every time I take a
wrong step it's a mistake."

It has to be seen
              as a great adventure.

I don't know a more effective way to
be with fear than to be still with it
in compassionate awareness.

For me, compassionate awareness is
most simply experienced in a meditation
practice.

A period of solitude and silence each
day helps us to realize that
     silence,
     stillness,
     compassion,

are who we truly are, are our true
nature, and that compassion
            is far greater
              and more powerful
               than fear.

If I want to be free,
I must find the courage
and the willingness
to be still

and face the fear that arises
when I attempt to come back
to my Self.